MONEY MASTERY

ACHIEVING FINANCIAL FREEDOM AT ANY AGE

ANURAG YADAV

Made with ♥ on the Notion Press Platform
www.notionpress.com

Contents

Contents

Foreword

It is my pleasure to introduce "Money Mastery: Achieving Financial Freedom at Any Age", a comprehensive guide to achieving financial independence in your 20s. This book is an invaluable resource for anyone looking to take control of their finances and achieve financial freedom.

In this book, the authors cover a wide range of topics, from setting financial goals and creating a budget, to managing expenses, increasing income, tracking progress, and staying motivated. They also delve into the importance of savings and investing, managing debt, building an emergency fund, and understanding insurance. The authors provide a thorough explanation of each topic, with clear examples and actionable advice.

One of the key strengths of this book is the attention given to the unique challenges that young people face when it comes to money management. The authors understand that in your 20s, you may be starting your career, paying off student loans, and trying to save for the future all at the same time. They provide practical strategies for navigating these challenges and achieving financial freedom.I believe that this book will be a valuable resource for anyone looking to take control of their finances and achieve financial freedom. The authors have done an excellent job of presenting complex financial concepts in an easy-to-understand manner. I highly recommend "Mastering Money in Your 20s: Achieving Financial Freedom" to anyone looking to take charge of their financial future.

Preface

Welcome to "Money Mastery: Achieving Financial Freedom at Any Age", a comprehensive guide to achieving financial independence at any age. In this book, we cover everything from setting financial goals and creating a budget, to managing expenses, increasing income, tracking progress, and staying motivated. We also delve into the importance of savings and investing, managing debt, building an emergency fund, and understanding insurance.

The book is divided into several chapters, each dedicated to a specific topic such as setting financial goals, creating a budget, managing expenses, increasing income, tracking progress and staying motivated, types of savings accounts, types of investments, compound interest, risk diversification, asset allocation, student loans, credit card debt, car loans, strategies for paying off debt, avoiding common mistakes, importance of an emergency fund, how to build an emergency fund, types of insurance, and how to choose the right insurance plan.

We also provide a chapter on long-term benefits of financial freedom and taking action towards financial independence, including recommended resources for further learning.

We understand that achieving financial independence can be overwhelming, but with the right knowledge and strategies, it is possible to achieve. This book is designed to provide readers with the information and tools they need to make informed decisions about their money and achieve financial independence.

We hope that this book serves as a valuable resource for anyone looking to achieve financial freedom in their 20s, and we wish you all the best in your journey towards financial independence.

Acknowledgements

Writing this book has been an incredible journey, and there are many people who have played a vital role in making it happen.

First and foremost, we would like to thank our readers for choosing this book and for taking the time to read it. We hope that the information and strategies outlined in this book will help you achieve financial freedom at any stage of your life.

We would like to extend our gratitude to our families, friends and colleagues for their support and encouragement throughout the writing process. Their unwavering belief in us was a constant source of motivation.

We would also like to thank our editor and proofreader, who helped us to make this book as clear and concise as possible. Their feedback and suggestions were invaluable.

Finally, we would like to express our gratitude to all the experts and authors who have written on the subject of personal finance and investing. Their work has provided us with a wealth of knowledge and has served as the foundation for this book.

This book is the result of all their support, guidance, and hard work. We are forever grateful.

CHAPTER ONE

SETTING THE FOUNDATION FOR FINANCIAL FREEDOM"

Importance of financial freedom

Financial freedom is a term that is often thrown around, but it is important to understand the true meaning and importance of achieving it. Financial freedom is the state of having enough wealth to live on without having to actively work for a living. It means having the ability to live the life you want, free from the constraints of worrying about money.

One of the most important aspects of financial freedom is the ability to live without stress and worry. When you are financially free, you don't have to worry about how you are going to pay your bills or whether you will be able to retire comfortably. You can sleep well at night knowing that your finances are in order and that you have the means to support yourself and your family.

Another important aspect of financial freedom is the ability to make choices. When you are financially free, you have the ability to make choices about how you want to live your life. You can choose to work, or not work, and you can choose to spend your time doing the things that you enjoy. This freedom allows you to live a life that is fulfilling and meaningful.

Achieving financial freedom is not easy, but it is possible. It takes hard work, discipline, and the ability to make smart financial decisions. The first step is to create a budget and stick to it. This will help you to understand where your money is going and where you can cut expenses. The next step is to start saving and investing. This will help you to build wealth and achieve financial freedom.

It's also important to invest in yourself, by learning more about financial literacy and to become more financially savvy. This includes understanding basic financial concepts, such as compound interest, risk diversification, and asset allocation, as well as understanding the different types of savings accounts and investments that are available.

Managing debt is also crucial to achieving financial freedom. This means paying off any outstanding debts as soon as possible, and avoiding taking on new debt if possible. It's also important to have an emergency fund, so that you have a financial safety net to fall back on in case of unexpected expenses.

Insurance is another important aspect of financial freedom. Having the right insurance coverage can help protect you from financial ruin in case of unexpected events, such as accidents or illnesses.

Achieving financial freedom is not a one-time event. It's a journey, and it requires ongoing effort and discipline. But the rewards are well worth it. When you are financially free, you have the freedom to live your life on your own terms and to pursue your dreams. So start taking the steps towards financial freedom today, and enjoy the peace of mind and freedom that it brings.

Setting financial goals

Setting financial goals is an essential step in achieving financial freedom. Financial goals provide a clear direction and purpose for your money, and give you something to work towards. Without financial goals, it can be easy to waste money on unnecessary expenses or to get caught up in the rat race of trying to keep up with others.

The first step in setting financial goals is to determine what is important to you. What do you want to achieve in the short-term and long-term? Do you want to buy a house, start a business, pay off debt, or save for retirement? Once you have a clear idea of what you want to achieve, you can start to create specific and measurable goals.

For example, if your goal is to buy a house, you can set a specific goal of saving a certain amount of money for a down payment within a specific time frame. Or if your goal is to pay off debt, you can set a specific goal of paying off a certain amount of debt within a specific time frame.

It's important to make sure your goals are realistic and attainable. Setting goals that are too ambitious can be demotivating, and can lead to giving up on them. It's important to break down big goals into smaller, more manageable goals that can be achieved in the short-term.

It's also important to set both short-term and long-term goals. Short-term goals provide immediate satisfaction and can help to keep you motivated, while long-term goals help to keep you focused on the bigger picture. Short-term goals can also help to provide the stepping-stones to achieving your long-term goals.

Another important aspect of setting financial goals is to create a plan to achieve them. This means creating a budget, and allocating your money towards your goals. It also means creating a timeline and tracking your progress, so you can see how close you are to achieving your goals.

To further increase the chances of achieving your financial goals, it's important to be accountable to someone else. It could be a friend, family member or financial advisor. This can help to keep you on track and motivated.

It's also important to have a positive attitude and to be flexible in your approach. Sometimes things don't go as planned, and it's important to be able to adjust your goals and plans as needed.

Setting financial goals is an ongoing process. It's important to regularly review your goals and progress, and to adjust them as needed. This can help to ensure that your goals remain relevant and aligned with your current financial situation.

In conclusion, setting financial goals is an essential step in achieving financial freedom. It provides a clear direction and purpose for your money, and gives you something to work towards. By setting specific and measurable goals, creating a plan to achieve them, staying accountable and having a positive attitude, you increase the chances of achieving your financial goals.

CHAPTER TWO

Money Mindset: The Key to Budgeting and Expense Management

Creating a budget

Creating a budget is a critical step in achieving financial freedom. A budget is a plan for how you will spend your money, and it helps you to understand where your money is going and where you can cut expenses. Without a budget, it can be easy to overspend and find yourself in a difficult financial situation.

The first step in creating a budget is to gather all of your financial information. This includes your income, expenses, and debts. It's important to be honest and realistic when gathering this information, as this will help to ensure that your budget is accurate.

Once you have all of your financial information, you can start to create a list of your income and expenses. This will help you to understand where your money is going and where you can cut expenses. It's important to be thorough and to include all of your income and expenses, including fixed expenses such as rent or mortgage, and variable expenses such as groceries or entertainment.

After you have a list of your income and expenses, you can start to create a budget. This is done by allocating your income towards your expenses. It's important to make sure that your expenses do not exceed your income, and to prioritize your expenses in terms of importance.

It's also important to set financial goals when creating a budget. This will help to ensure that your budget is aligned with your financial goals and that you are allocating your money towards things that are important to you.

It's also important to review and adjust your budget regularly. This will help to ensure that it stays relevant and aligned with your current financial situation. This can also help you to identify areas where you can cut expenses or increase income.

Creating a budget can be difficult, but there are many tools and resources available to help. Budgeting apps, spreadsheet templates, and financial advisors are all great resources that can help to make the process easier.

In conclusion, creating a budget is a critical step in achieving financial freedom. It helps you to understand where your money is going and where you can cut expenses. It's important to be honest and realistic when gathering financial information, and to prioritize expenses in terms of importance. Setting financial goals and regularly reviewing and adjusting your budget can help to ensure that it stays relevant and aligned with your current financial situation. With the right tools and resources, creating a budget can be a manageable and rewarding process.

Managing expenses

Managing expenses is a critical step in achieving financial freedom. It involves understanding where your money is going, and making conscious decisions about how you spend it. Without proper expense management, it can be easy to overspend and find yourself in a difficult financial situation.

The first step in managing expenses is to understand where your money is going. This involves creating a budget and tracking your expenses. This will help you to understand your spending habits and identify areas where you can cut expenses.

It's important to be realistic and honest when tracking your expenses, as this will help to ensure that your budget is accurate. It's also important to include all of your expenses, including fixed expenses such as rent or mortgage, and variable expenses such as groceries or entertainment.

Once you have a clear understanding of where your money is going, you can start to make conscious decisions about how you spend it. This means prioritizing your expenses in terms of importance and cutting out unnecessary expenses.

It's important to set financial goals when managing expenses. This will help to ensure that your expenses are aligned with your financial goals and that you are spending your money on things that are important to you.

It's also important to review and adjust your expenses regularly. This will help to ensure that they stay relevant and aligned with your current financial situation. This can also help you to identify areas where you can cut expenses or increase income.

Managing expenses can be difficult, but there are many tools and resources available to help. Budgeting apps, spreadsheet templates, and financial advisors are all great resources that can help to make the process easier.

One of the effective ways to manage expenses is to establish a system of payment. Instead of using credit cards, which can easily lead to overspending, it's better to use cash or debit cards. This way, you can keep better track of your expenses, and avoid overspending.

Increasing income

Increasing income is an important step in achieving financial freedom. It involves finding ways to bring in more money, in order to have more resources to put towards your financial goals and expenses. Without increasing income, it can be difficult to achieve financial freedom, as expenses tend to increase over time.

The first step in increasing income is to understand your current income streams. This includes identifying your primary source of income, as well as any additional sources of income, such as investments or side hustles. It's important to be honest and realistic when assessing your income, as this will help to ensure that your plan for increasing income is accurate.

Once you have a clear understanding of your current income streams, you can start to identify ways to increase them. This can include asking for a raise at work, negotiating a better salary when starting a new job, or starting a side hustle.

It's important to set financial goals when increasing income. This will help to ensure that your efforts to increase income are aligned with your financial goals and that you are focusing on ways to bring in more money that align with your interests and skills.

It's also important to be creative and open-minded when looking for ways to increase income. This can include taking on freelance work, renting out a spare room on Airbnb, or starting an online business.

It's also important to regularly review and adjust your income streams. This will help to ensure that they stay relevant and aligned with your current financial situation. This can also help you to identify areas where you can increase income or cut expenses.

Increasing income can be difficult, but there are many tools and resources available to help. Networking, taking classes, and learning about different business opportunities are all great resources that can help to make the process easier.

In conclusion, increasing income is an important step in achieving financial freedom. It involves finding ways to bring in more money, in order to have more resources to put towards your financial goals and expenses. It's important to set financial goals, be creative, open-minded, and to regularly review and adjust your income streams. With the right tools and resources, increasing income can be a manageable and rewarding process.

Tracking progress and staying motivated

Tracking progress and staying motivated are critical steps in achieving financial freedom. Without tracking progress and staying motivated, it can be easy to lose sight of your goals and to give up on your journey to financial freedom.

The first step in tracking progress and staying motivated is to set specific and measurable financial goals. This will provide a clear direction and purpose for your money, and give you something to work towards. It's important to be realistic and honest when setting goals, as this will help to ensure that they are attainable.

Once you have set your financial goals, it's important to create a plan to achieve them. This includes creating a budget, allocating your money towards your goals, and creating a timeline. It's also important to track your progress, so you can see how close you are to achieving your goals.

Tracking progress and staying motivated also involves staying accountable. This means sharing your financial goals and progress with someone else, whether it's a friend, family member, or financial advisor. This can help to keep you on track and motivated, and can provide a valuable source of support and encouragement.

It's also important to have a positive attitude and to be flexible in your approach. Sometimes things don't go as planned, and it's important to be able to adjust your goals and plans as needed. This can help to keep you motivated and focused on your journey to financial freedom.

It's also important to celebrate your successes along the way. Achieving financial goals, no matter how small, is a significant accomplishment and should be celebrated. Recognizing and rewarding yourself for your progress can help to keep you motivated and focused on the bigger picture.

Another important aspect of tracking progress and staying motivated is to continuously educate yourself on personal finance and money management. Staying informed and up-to-date with the latest financial trends and best practices can help you make better financial decisions and achieve your goals faster.

It's also important to stay motivated by reminding yourself of the end goal. Visualize the future you want for yourself and your family, and remind yourself of the benefits that come with financial freedom. This can help to keep you motivated and focused when things get tough.

In conclusion, tracking progress and staying motivated are critical steps in achieving financial freedom. It involves setting specific and measurable financial goals, creating a plan to achieve them, staying accountable, having a positive attitude, and continuously educating yourself on personal finance and money management. By staying focused and motivated, you increase the chances of achieving your financial goals and enjoying the benefits of financial freedom.

CHAPTER THREE

Investing for Beginners: A Guide to Saving and Investing for Financial Freedom

Types of savings accounts

Saving money is an essential step in achieving financial freedom. It helps to build wealth and provides a financial safety net for unexpected expenses. One of the most effective ways to save money is by using a savings account. Savings accounts are offered by banks and other financial institutions, and they provide a secure and convenient way to save money.

There are several different types of savings accounts available, each with their own unique features and benefits. The most common types of savings accounts include:

1. Traditional savings account: This is the most basic type of savings account. It typically offers a low interest rate, but it is easy to open and manage. This account is ideal for people who want a simple and convenient way to save money.
2. High-yield savings account: This type of savings account offers a higher interest rate than traditional savings accounts. This is because they often require a higher minimum deposit and a higher balance to maintain the account. This account is ideal for people who have a larger amount of money to save and want to earn more interest on their savings.
3. Money market account: This type of account offers a higher interest rate than traditional savings accounts, and it is also FDIC-insured. Money market accounts also often have check-writing capabilities, and limited check-writing capabilities, and limited check-writing privileges, making them a good option for saving money while also having access to it for liquidity needs.
4. Certificates of Deposit (CDs): These are savings accounts where you deposit a certain amount of money for a fixed period of time and agree not to withdraw it until the term

ends. CDs typically offer a higher interest rate than traditional savings accounts, but you'll face penalties if you need to withdraw your money before the term ends.

5. Online savings accounts: These accounts are offered by online banks and typically offer higher interest rates than traditional savings accounts. They also often have lower fees and minimum deposit requirements.

When choosing a savings account, it's important to consider the interest rate, minimum deposit requirements, fees, and access to your funds. It's also important to consider your personal savings goals and how you plan to use the account. For example, if you plan to use the account as an emergency fund, you may want to choose a savings account with easy access to your funds. If you're saving for a long-term goal, such as retirement, a higher interest rate account may be more beneficial.

It's also important to shop around and compare different savings accounts to find the one that best suits your needs. Many banks and financial institutions offer online tools and calculators to help you compare different accounts and estimate the interest you can earn over time.

It's important to also consider the safety and security of the institution where you open your account. Look for FDIC-insured institutions and make sure the institution is reputable and established.

In conclusion, savings accounts are an essential tool for achieving financial freedom. There are several different types of savings accounts available, each with their own unique features and benefits. It's important to consider the interest rate, minimum deposit requirements, fees, and access to your funds, as well as your personal savings goals when choosing a savings account.

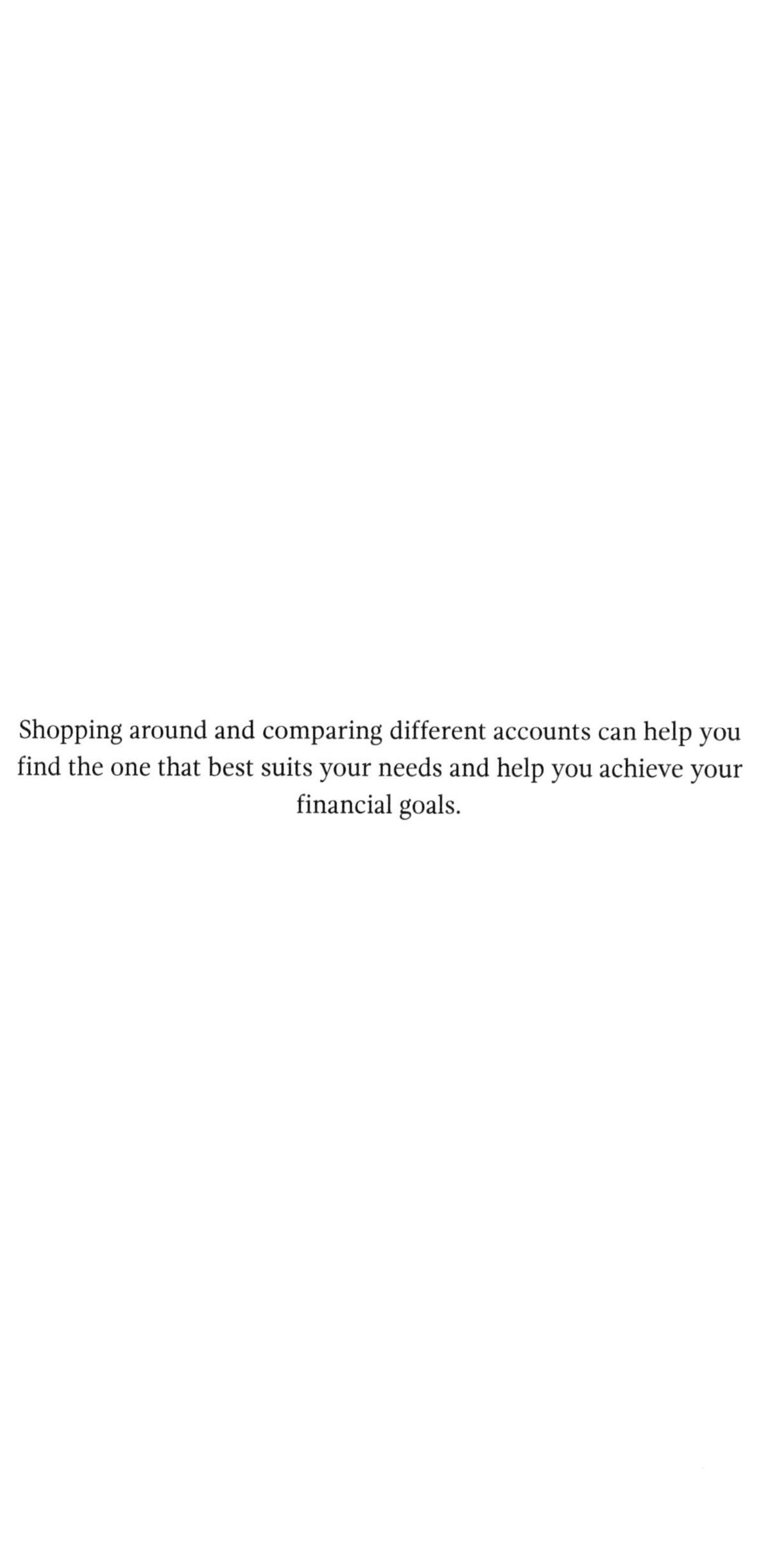

Shopping around and comparing different accounts can help you find the one that best suits your needs and help you achieve your financial goals.

Types of investments

Investing is a key component of achieving financial freedom, as it helps to grow your wealth and provides a means for achieving long-term financial goals. There are many different types of investments available, each with their own unique features and benefits. Understanding the different types of investments can help you make informed decisions about how to allocate your money and achieve your financial goals.

1. Stock market investments: This type of investment involves buying shares of stock in a publicly traded company. The value of the stock can increase or decrease based on the performance of the company and overall market conditions. Stock market investments can be volatile in the short term, but they have the potential to provide high returns over the long term.
2. Bonds: A bond is a debt investment, where an investor loans money to a corporation, municipality, or government in exchange for regular interest payments and the return of the principal at maturity. Bonds are considered to be less risky than stocks, but they also generally offer lower returns.
3. Real estate: Investing in real estate involves purchasing property with the goal of earning rental income or profiting from the appreciation of the property value. Real estate investments can be a good way to generate passive income, but they also require a significant amount of capital and can be risky.
4. Mutual funds: These are professionally managed investment portfolios that pools money from multiple investors to purchase a diverse range of securities. Mutual funds offer a convenient way for investors to gain exposure to a variety of stocks, bonds, or other securities, and they can be less risky

than investing in individual securities.

5. Exchange-traded funds (ETFs): These are similar to mutual funds

Compound interest

Compound interest is a powerful tool that can help to grow your wealth over time. It is the process of earning interest on interest, and it can have a significant impact on the growth of your investments. Understanding the concept of compound interest and how it works is essential for achieving financial freedom.

Compound interest is calculated on the original principal amount and the accumulated interest from previous periods. The longer the money is invested, the more interest it earns, and the more the interest earns interest. This means that the longer the money is invested, the more it will grow.

For example, if you invest $1000 at a 5% annual interest rate, after the first year, you will have earned $50 in interest (5% of $1000). In the second year, the interest is calculated on the original $1000 plus the $50 in interest earned in the first year, resulting in $52.50 in interest earned. By the third year, you would have earned $55.13 in interest, and so on.

The power of compound interest can be seen over a long period of time. For example, if you invest $1000 at 5% interest for 20 years, your investment would have grown to $1,628.89, but if you had invested it for 40 years, it would have grown to $2,653.33.

Compound interest can be a powerful tool for achieving financial freedom, but it also highlights the importance of starting to invest as early as possible. The earlier you start investing, the more time your money has to grow and the more you will benefit from compound interest.

Additionally, it's important to choose investments that compound interest, for example, a savings account, mutual funds, bonds, and some stocks. These investments compound interest over time and can help grow your wealth faster.

In conclusion, Compound interest is a powerful tool that can help to grow your wealth over time. It is the process of earning interest on interest, and it can have a significant impact on the growth of your investments. Starting to invest as early as possible, choosing investments that compound interest, and having a long-term investment horizon are the key to benefit from the power of compound interest and achieve financial freedom.

Risk diversification

Risk diversification is a strategy used to spread investments among different asset classes, sectors, and individual securities to reduce the overall risk in a portfolio. The idea behind risk diversification is that by spreading investments across different types of assets, an investor can reduce the impact of a potential loss in any one particular asset class. This can help to protect against market volatility and decrease the likelihood of a portfolio losing value.

One of the most important benefits of diversification is that it can help to reduce the overall risk in a portfolio. By spreading investments across different asset classes, investors can reduce the impact of a potential loss in any one particular asset class. For example, if an investor has a portfolio that is heavily invested in the stock market, and the stock market experiences a significant downturn, the value of their portfolio will likely decrease as well. However, if the same investor has diversified their portfolio to include other asset classes such as bonds, real estate, and cash, the impact of the stock market downturn on their portfolio will likely be less severe.

Another benefit of diversification is that it can help to increase the potential for returns. When an investor diversifies their portfolio, they are able to invest in a variety of assets that may perform differently in different market conditions. This means that even if one asset class is underperforming, another asset class in the portfolio may be performing well, which can help to offset any potential losses.

Diversification can also be achieved by spreading investments across different sectors and individual securities within the same asset class. For example, instead of investing all of the money in one stock, an investor can spread their investments across several stocks in the same sector. This can help to reduce the risk of a loss if one particular stock underperforms.

It's important to note that diversification does not guarantee a profit or protect against loss. Diversifying does not mean spreading your investment equally, it's about spreading it among different types of assets that have different risk and return characteristics.

In conclusion, Risk diversification is a strategy used to spread investments among different asset classes, sectors, and individual securities to reduce the overall risk in a portfolio. Diversification can help to reduce the overall risk in a portfolio, increase the potential for returns, and protect against market volatility. It's important to note that diversification does not guarantee a profit or protect against loss, and it's important to choose the right mix of assets that align with your risk tolerance and financial goals.

Asset allocation

Asset allocation is the process of dividing an investment portfolio among different asset categories, such as stocks, bonds, and cash. The goal of asset allocation is to create a balance of risk and return that aligns with an individual's investment goals, risk tolerance, and time horizon. By diversifying investments across different asset classes, investors can reduce their overall risk and increase the potential for returns.

When creating an asset allocation plan, it's important to consider your risk tolerance, investment goals, and time horizon. For example, if you have a low risk tolerance and a short-term investment horizon, you may want to allocate a larger portion of your portfolio to cash and fixed-income investments, such as bonds. On the other hand, if you have a high risk tolerance and a long-term investment horizon, you may want to allocate a larger portion of your portfolio to stocks and other growth-oriented investments.

It's also important to regularly review and rebalance your asset allocation. As different asset classes perform differently over time, the mix of assets in your portfolio may become unbalanced. For example, if the stock market is performing well, the value of your stocks may increase, which could cause your portfolio to become overweight in stocks. To maintain a proper balance of risk and return, it's important to periodically sell some of the assets that have grown in value and reallocate them to other asset classes that have underperformed.

Asset allocation can also be achieved by spreading investments across different sectors and individual securities within the same asset class. For example, instead of investing all of the money in one stock, an investor can spread their investments across several stocks in the same sector. This can help to reduce the risk of a loss if one particular stock underperforms.

It's important to note that asset allocation does not guarantee a profit or protect against loss. It's also important to consider your personal financial situation, such as your tax situation, investment goals, and time horizon when making decisions about asset allocation.

In conclusion, Asset allocation is the process of dividing an investment portfolio among different assetcategories, such as stocks, bonds, and cash, to create a balance of risk and return that aligns with an individual's investment goals, risk tolerance, and time horizon. By diversifying investments across different asset classes, investors can reduce their overall risk and increase the potential for returns. When creating an asset allocation plan, it's important to consider your risk tolerance, investment goals, and time horizon. It's also important to regularly review and rebalance your asset allocation to maintain a proper balance of risk and return. It's important to note that asset allocation does not guarantee a profit or protect against loss and it's important to consider your personal financial situation when making decisions about asset allocation. Additionally, Asset allocation should be done in conjunction with proper risk management techniques, and it's essential to have a well thought out financial plan in place.

CHAPTER FOUR

Debt Management Mastery: Achieving Financial Stability

Student loans

Student loans are a type of loan designed to help students pay for their education. These loans are typically issued by the government or private lenders, and they can be used to cover the cost of tuition, fees, room and board, and other expenses associated with attending college or graduate school. With the rising cost of education, student loans have become an increasingly common way for students to finance their education.

One of the main advantages of student loans is that they provide access to education for those who may not have the financial means to pay for it outright. This is particularly important for low-income students, who may not have the resources to pay for college without the help of student loans.

Student loans come in two main types: federal student loans and private student loans. Federal student loans are issued and guaranteed by the U.S. government and typically have lower interest rates and more favorable repayment terms than private student loans. Examples of federal student loans include Stafford loans and Perkins loans. Private student loans are issued by banks, credit unions, and other private lenders and typically have higher interest rates and less favorable repayment terms than federal student loans.

When considering student loans, it's important to understand the terms and conditions of the loan, including the interest rate, repayment period, and any fees associated with the loan. It's also important to consider the total amount of debt that will be incurred, and the potential impact on the student's future financial situation.

Repaying student loans can be a significant financial burden for many graduates. It's important to understand the repayment options available, such as income-driven repayment plans, which base the monthly payment on the borrower's income, and loan forgiveness programs, which may forgive the remaining balance of the loan after a certain period of time.

It's also important to be aware that defaulting on student loans can have serious consequences, including wage garnishment, tax refund interception, and damage to credit score.

In conclusion, student loans are a type of loan designed to help students pay for their education. They can be a useful tool for financing a college education, but it's important to understand the terms and conditions of the loan, the potential impact on the student's future financial situation, and the repayment options available. It's also important to be aware of the potential consequences of defaulting on student loans. It's always important to consider all options, including grants, scholarships, and work-study before taking on student loan debt.

Credit card debt

Credit card debt is a type of consumer debt that is incurred through the use of credit cards. It occurs when an individual borrows money from a credit card company and is required to pay it back, along with interest and other charges. Credit card debt can be a major financial burden for many individuals, and it's important to understand the potential risks and consequences of incurring this type of debt.

One of the main risks of credit card debt is that it can quickly spiral out of control if not managed properly. Credit card companies often offer revolving credit, which means that the borrower can continue to borrow against the credit limit as long as they make the minimum payments. This can make it easy for borrowers to accumulate a large amount of debt without realizing it. Additionally, credit card interest rates are often quite high, which can make it difficult to pay off the debt in a timely manner.

Another risk of credit card debt is that it can have a negative impact on an individual's credit score. A high level of credit card debt can indicate to lenders that an individual is a high-risk borrower, which can make it more difficult to obtain loans or credit in the future. Additionally, missed or late payments on credit card debt can have a negative impact on an individual's credit score.

To avoid falling into credit card debt, it's important to use credit cards responsibly. This includes only charging what can be paid off in full each month, paying bills on time and in full, and keeping a close eye on credit card balances. It's also important to be mindful of the interest rates and fees associated with credit cards, and to consider alternative forms of payment, such as cash or debit cards.

If an individual finds themselves in credit card debt, there are steps that can be taken to manage and pay off the debt. This includes creating a budget, consolidating or transferring the debt to a card with a lower interest rate, and negotiating with credit card companies to reduce or eliminate interest charges.

In conclusion, credit card debt is a type of consumer debt that is incurred through the use of credit cards. It can be a major financial burden for many individuals and it's important to understand the potential risks and consequences of incurring this type of debt. It's crucial to use credit cards responsibly, to be mindful of interest rates and fees, and to have a plan to manage and pay off the debt. It's also important to consider alternative forms of payment, such as cash or debit cards, and to seek professional financial advice if necessary.

Car loans

A car loan is a type of personal loan that is used to purchase a vehicle. These loans are typically issued by banks, credit unions, and other financial institutions, and they can be used to purchase new or used cars, trucks, and other vehicles. Car loans can be a convenient way for individuals to purchase a vehicle, but it's important to understand the terms and conditions of the loan, as well as the potential risks and consequences of incurring this type of debt.

One of the main advantages of car loans is that they allow individuals to purchase a vehicle that they may not be able to afford outright. This can be particularly beneficial for those who need a reliable vehicle for work or other essential purposes. Additionally, car loans can be a good way to build credit, as long as the loans are paid back on time and in full.

However, car loans can also be a significant financial burden if not managed properly. Car loans typically have longer terms than other types of loans, such as personal loans or credit card debt, which means that the borrower is required to make payments for a longer period of time. Additionally, car loans often have higher interest rates than other types of loans, which can make it more difficult to pay off the debt in a timely manner.

When considering a car loan, it's important to understand the terms and conditions of the loan, including the interest rate, repayment period, and any fees associated with the loan. It's also important to consider the total amount of debt that will be incurred and the potential impact on the individual's future financial situation.

It's important to note that defaulting on a car loan can have serious consequences, such as repossession of the vehicle, damage to credit score, and legal action.

To avoid falling into debt with a car loan, it's important to

consider all options before making a purchase. This includes researching different makes and models of vehicles, shopping around for the best interest rates, and considering the total cost of ownership, including maintenance, insurance, and fuel costs. It's also important to consider the possibility of purchasing a used or certified pre-owned vehicle, which can be a more cost-effective option.

When applying for a car loan, it's important to have a good credit score and a stable income. This can increase the chances of being approved for the loan and can also help to secure a lower interest rate. It's also important to be aware of the potential impact of a car loan on your budget and to ensure that the loan payments can be made on time and in full.

If an individual finds themselves in debt with a car loan, there are steps that can be taken to manage and pay off the debt. This includes creating a budget, consolidating or refinancing the loan to a lower interest rate, and negotiating with the lender to reduce or eliminate interest charges.

In conclusion, a car loan is a type of personal loan that is used to purchase a vehicle. These loans can be a convenient way for individuals to purchase a vehicle, but it's important to understand the terms and conditions of the loan, as well as the potential risks and consequences of incurring this type of debt. It's crucial to consider all options before making a purchase, to have a good credit score and a stable income when applying for a car loan and to have a plan to manage and pay off the debt if necessary. It's also important to be aware of the potential impact of a car loan on your budget and to ensure that the loan payments can be made on time and in full.

Strategies for paying off debt

Paying off debt can be a challenging task, but there are several strategies that can be used to help individuals achieve this goal. It's important to have a plan in place and to be disciplined in following through with the plan. Here are some strategies for paying off debt:

1. Prioritize high-interest debt: High-interest debt, such as credit card debt, can be particularly burdensome because of the high interest rates. Prioritizing these types of debts and paying them off first can save a significant amount of money in interest charges over time.
2. Create a budget: Creating a budget can help individuals to better understand their spending habits and make adjustments as necessary to allocate more money towards debt repayment. A budget can also help to identify areas where expenses can be reduced in order to free up more money to put towards paying off debt.
3. Increase income: Increasing income can help to accelerate the debt repayment process. This can be achieved through a variety of means such as working overtime, getting a second job, or starting a side business.
4. Consolidate debt: Consolidating debt can make it easier to manage and can also lower the overall interest rate. This can be achieved by taking out a consolidation loan or by transferring high-interest credit card balances to a card with a lower interest rate.
5. Use the snowball method: The snowball method involves paying off the smallest debt first and then moving on to the next one. This can provide a sense of accomplishment and motivation to continue paying off debt.

6. Use the avalanche method: The avalanche method involves paying off the highest interest debt first, regardless of the balance. This can save more money in the long run, but it may not provide the same sense of accomplishment as the snowball method.
7. Seek professional advice: If an individual is struggling to pay off debt, they may want to consider seeking professional advice from a financial advisor or credit counselor. These professionals can provide personalized advice and strategies for paying off debt, and can also help to negotiate with creditors for more favorable terms or to set up a debt management plan.
8. Avoid taking on new debt: While paying off debt, it's important to avoid taking on new debt. This can be achieved by avoiding using credit cards, limiting the number of loans, and making a conscious effort to save money before making any big purchases.
9. Automate payments: Automating payments can help to ensure that the debt is paid on time and in full. This can also help to avoid late fees and penalties, which can add to the overall debt.
10. Stay motivated: Paying off debt can be a long and challenging process, but it's important to stay motivated. This can be achieved by setting small and realistic goals, keeping track of progress, and rewarding oneself for reaching milestones.

In conclusion, paying off debt can be challenging, but it's important to have a plan in place and to be disciplined in following through with the plan. Prioritizing high-interest debt, creating a budget, increasing income, consolidating debt, using the snowball or avalanche method, seeking professional advice, avoiding taking on new debt, automating payments, and staying motivated, are some strategies that can be used to help individuals achieve the goal of paying off debt. It's important to remember that paying off debt will require time and effort, but the end result of becoming debt-free will be worth it in the long run

Avoiding common mistakes

Avoiding common mistakes is an important part of achieving financial success. Here are some common mistakes that individuals make and strategies for avoiding them:

1. Not creating a budget: Not creating a budget is one of the most common mistakes people make. A budget can help individuals to better understand their spending habits and make adjustments as necessary to allocate more money towards savings and debt repayment.
2. Not having an emergency fund: Not having an emergency fund is another common mistake. An emergency fund is a savings account that is set aside for unexpected expenses such as medical emergencies, car repairs, or job loss. It's important to have enough money saved to cover at least three to six months of living expenses.
3. Not saving for retirement: Not saving for retirement is a common mistake that can have serious consequences. It's important to start saving for retirement as early as possible, and to make sure that contributions are being made to a retirement account on a regular basis.
4. Not paying off high-interest debt: Not paying off high-interest debt is another common mistake. High-interest debt, such as credit card debt, can be particularly burdensome because of the high interest rates. Prioritizing these types of debts and paying them off first can save a significant amount of money in interest charges over time.
5. Not shopping around for the best interest rates: Not shopping around for the best interest rates is a common mistake when it comes to loans, credit cards, and mortgages. It's important to compare the interest rates and terms of different financial products to ensure that the best deal is being obtained.

6. Not having insurance: Not having insurance is another common mistake. Insurance can provide protection for individuals and their families in case of accidents, illness, or death. It's important to have enough insurance to cover potential losses.
7. Not understanding the terms and conditions of financial products: Not understanding the terms and conditions of financial products is a common mistake. It's important to read and understand the fine print of any financial product before making a decision.
8. Not reviewing credit report: Not reviewing credit report is another common mistake. Checking credit report regularly and correcting any errors can help maintain a good credit score, which can make it easier to obtain loans and credit in the future.

In conclusion, avoiding common mistakes is an important part of achieving financial success. It's important to create a budget, have an emergency fund, save for retirement, pay off high-interest debt, shop around for the best interest rates, have insurance, understand the terms and conditions of financial products and review credit report.

CHAPTER FIVE

The Financial Safety Net: Building an Emergency Fund

Importance of an emergency fund

An emergency fund is a savings account that is set aside for unexpected expenses such as medical emergencies, car repairs, or job loss. It is a crucial aspect of personal finance and provides a safety net for individuals and their families in case of unexpected events. Here are some reasons why an emergency fund is important:

1. Protection against unexpected expenses: An emergency fund provides a safety net for individuals and their families in case of unexpected events, such as medical emergencies, home repairs, or loss of job. This can help to reduce the financial stress and burden that can be caused by unexpected expenses.
2. Avoiding debt: An emergency fund can help individuals to avoid going into debt, such as credit card debt, to pay for unexpected expenses. This can help to improve an individual's credit score and overall financial health.
3. Financial stability: An emergency fund can provide a sense of financial stability and security. Knowing that there is money set aside for unexpected expenses can help to reduce stress and anxiety about money.
4. Independence: An emergency fund can provide financial independence. It gives individuals the ability to handle unexpected expenses without having to rely on others for financial assistance.
5. Meeting long-term financial goals: An emergency fund can also help individuals to meet long-term financial goals, such as saving for retirement or buying a home. By having an emergency fund, individuals can avoid dipping into their

savings or retirement accounts to pay for unexpected expenses, which can help to ensure that these long-term goals are met.

6. Flexibility: An emergency fund can provide flexibility in case of unexpected events, such as job loss or health issues. This can help individuals to avoid having to make hasty decisions and can give them time to make well thought-out decisions.
7. Peace of mind: Having an emergency fund can give individuals peace of mind knowing that they have a safety net in case of unexpected events.

It's recommended to have an emergency fund that covers at least three to six months of living expenses. Building an emergency fund takes time, but it's important to start saving as early as possible and to make regular contributions to the fund. It's also important to keep the emergency fund in a liquid account such as a savings account, so that the funds can be easily accessible in case of an emergency.

In conclusion, an emergency fund is a crucial aspect of personal finance and provides a safety net for individuals and their families in case of unexpected events. An emergency fund can help to reduce the financial stress and burden caused by unexpected expenses, avoid going into debt, provide financial stability and security, financial independence, meeting long-term financial goals, flexibility and peace of mind. It's recommended to have an emergency fund that covers at least three to six months of living expenses and to start saving as early as possible and to make regular contributions to the fund.

How to build an emergency fund

Building an emergency fund is an important step in achieving financial stability and security. An emergency fund is a savings account that is set aside for unexpected expenses such as medical emergencies, car repairs, or job loss. Here are some strategies for building an emergency fund:

Set a savings goal: The first step in building an emergency fund is to set a savings goal. It's recommended to have an emergency fund that covers at least three to six months of living expenses. This will provide a safety net for individuals and their families in case of unexpected events.

Create a budget: Creating a budget can help individuals to better understand their spending habits and make adjustments as necessary to allocate more money towards savings. By identifying areas where expenses can be reduced, individuals can free up more money to put towards building an emergency fund.

Increase income: Increasing income can also help accelerate the savings process. This can be achieved by working overtime, getting a second job, or starting a side business.

Automate savings: Automating savings can help to ensure that regular contributions are made to the emergency fund. This can be done by setting up automatic transfers from a checking account to a savings account on a regular basis.

Cut unnecessary expenses: Reviewing expenses and cutting unnecessary expenses can also help to free up more money to put towards building an emergency fund. This can include cutting back on subscriptions, memberships, or luxury items.

Reduce debt: Paying off high-interest debt can also help to free up more money to put towards building an emergency fund. This can be achieved by creating a plan for paying off debt, such as the snowball or avalanche method, and prioritizing high-interest debt.

Take advantage of windfalls: When individuals receive windfalls, such as a tax refund or bonus, they should consider putting the money towards building an emergency fund.

Keep the emergency fund in a liquid account: Once the emergency fund is built, it's important to keep the funds in a liquid account, such as a savings account, so that the funds can be easily accessible in case of an emergency.

Building an emergency fund takes time, but it's important to start saving as early as possible and to make regular contributions to the fund. It's also important to remember that building an emergency fund is an ongoing process and contributions should continue to be made to the fund on a regular basis.

In conclusion, building an emergency fund is an important step in achieving financial stability and security. It's recommended to have an emergency fund that covers at least three to six months of living expenses. Strategies for building an emergency fund include setting a savings goal, creating a budget, increasing income, automating savings, cutting unnecessary expenses, reducing debt, taking advantage of windfalls, and keeping the emergency fund in a liquid account. By following these strategies, individuals can create a safety net for themselves and their families in case of unexpected events. It's also important to remember that building an emergency fund is an ongoing process, and contributions should continue to be made to the fund on a regular basis. It's also important to keep the emergency fund separate from other savings or investment accounts, to avoid using it for non-

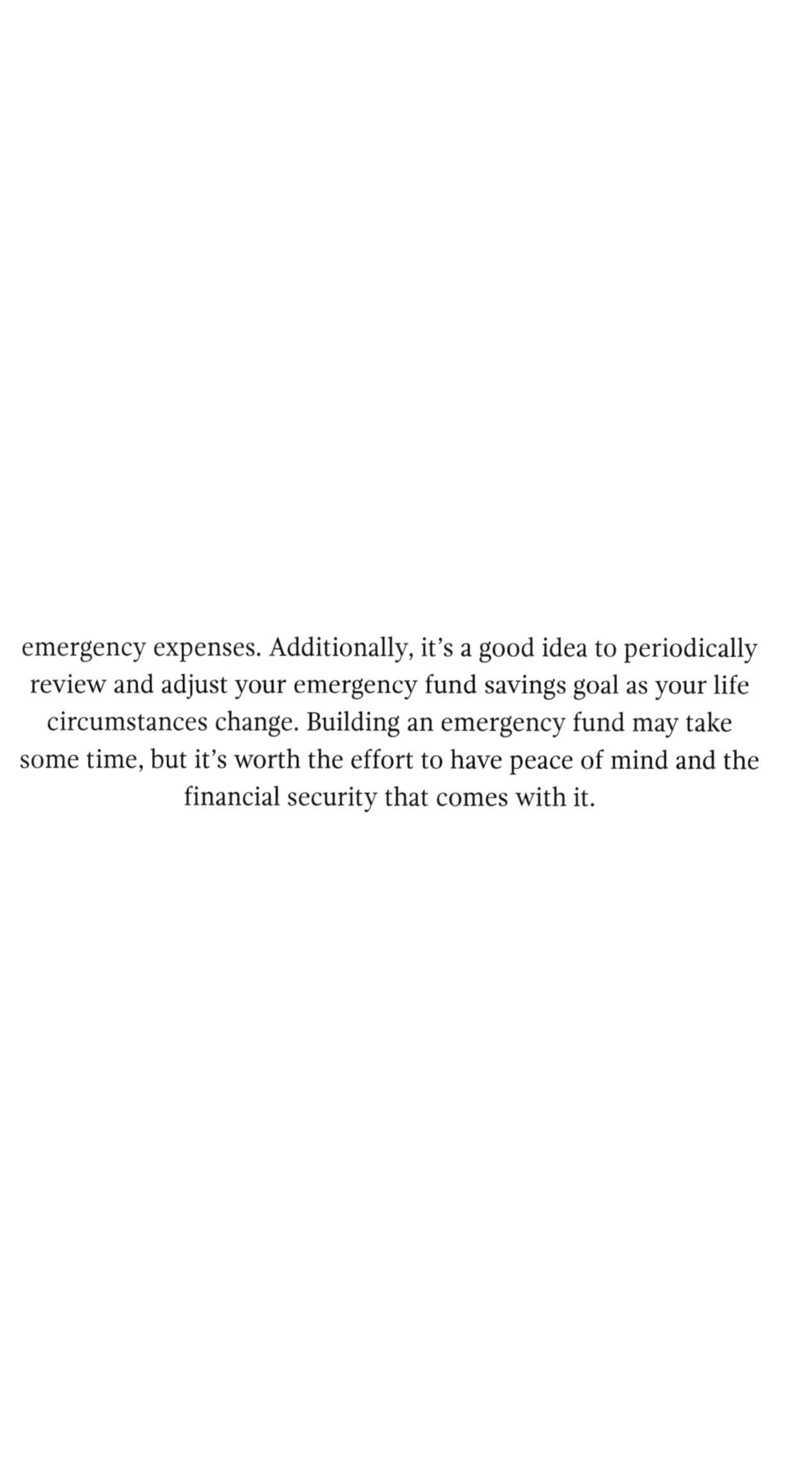

emergency expenses. Additionally, it's a good idea to periodically review and adjust your emergency fund savings goal as your life circumstances change. Building an emergency fund may take some time, but it's worth the effort to have peace of mind and the financial security that comes with it.

CHAPTER SIX

Risk Management: The Importance of Insurance

Types of insurance

Insurance is a crucial aspect of personal finance, as it can provide protection for individuals and their families in case of accidents, illness, or death. There are several types of insurance that individuals can consider, each with its own specific purpose and benefits. Here are some types of insurance to consider:

1. Health Insurance: Health insurance provides financial protection in case of medical expenses due to an illness or injury. Health insurance can be purchased through an employer, or through government-funded programs such as Medicaid and Medicare.
2. Life Insurance: Life insurance provides financial protection for an individual's family in case of the individual's death. The death benefit can be used to cover expenses such as funeral costs, outstanding debts, and living expenses for the individual's family.
3. Auto Insurance: Auto insurance provides financial protection in case of accidents involving an individual's car. Auto insurance can also provide protection against theft, vandalism and natural disasters.
4. Homeowners Insurance: Homeowners insurance provides financial protection in case of damage to an individual's home or personal property. This can include protection against natural disasters, fire, and theft.
5. Disability Insurance: Disability insurance provides financial protection in case of an individual's inability to work due to a disability. This can help to cover living expenses and other financial obligations while the individual is unable to work.
6. Long-term Care Insurance: Long-term care insurance provides financial protection in case of an individual's need for long-term care, such as in a nursing home or assisted living facility.

7. Umbrella Insurance: Umbrella insurance provides additional liability coverage beyond the limits of an individual's other insurance policies, such as auto or homeowners insurance.
8. Travel Insurance: Travel insurance provides financial protection in case of unexpected events such as trip cancellation, medical emergencies, lost baggage and more.

It's important to note that not all types of insurance will be necessary or even applicable to everyone. Factors such as age, health, lifestyle, and occupation all play a role in determining which types of insurance an individual may need. It's important to do research and to consult with insurance professionals to determine the appropriate types and amounts of insurance coverage.

In conclusion, Insurance is a crucial aspect of personal finance as it can provide protection for individuals and their families in case of accidents, illness, or death. There are several types of insurance such as Health Insurance, Life Insurance, Auto Insurance, Homeowners Insurance, Disability Insurance, Long-term Care Insurance, Umbrella Insurance, and Travel Insurance. It's important to determine the appropriate types and amount of insurance coverage by considering factors such as age, health, lifestyle, and occupation. It's also important to review and adjust insurance coverage as life circumstances change. It's important to do research and to consult with insurance professionals to understand the different types of insurance, their coverage and cost, as well as to make sure that you have enough coverage to protect yourself and your assets.

Additionally, it's important to understand the differences between different types of insurance, such as term life insurance and whole life insurance, and to select the one that best fits your needs. It's also important to review your insurance policies regularly and to compare them with other options to ensure that you're getting the best coverage at the best price.

In summary, insurance is an essential aspect of personal finance, it provides protection for individuals and their families in case of accidents, illness, or death. Different types of insurance are available such as health, life, auto, homeowner, disability, long-term care, umbrella and travel insurance. It's important to determine the appropriate types and amount of insurance coverage, review and adjust as life circumstances change, and consult with insurance professionals to ensure you have the right coverage to protect yourself and your assets.

How to choose the right insurance plan

Choosing the right insurance plan can be overwhelming, as there are many options available and each plan can have different levels of coverage and costs. It's important to understand the different types of insurance available and to select a plan that best fits an individual's needs. Here are some strategies for choosing the right insurance plan:

1. Assess your needs: The first step in choosing the right insurance plan is to assess your needs. This includes evaluating your current health status, lifestyle, occupation, and financial situation. This will help you to determine which types of insurance you need and the level of coverage that is appropriate for you.
2. Research different options: After assessing your needs, research different insurance options. Compare the coverage and costs of different plans, and look for any exclusions or limitations. It's also important to understand the differences between different types of insurance, such as term life insurance and whole life insurance.
3. Compare the benefits and costs: Compare the benefits and costs of different plans. Look for plans that provide the level of coverage you need at a price you can afford. It's also important to consider the out-of-pocket costs, such as deductibles and co-pays, as well as the network of providers.
4. Read the fine print: Carefully read and understand the terms and conditions of any insurance plan before making a decision. Make sure you understand the exclusions, limitations, and any pre-existing conditions that may not be covered.

5. Consult with a professional: Consult with an insurance professional to help you understand the different options available and to make sure that you are getting the best coverage for your needs.
6. Review and adjust coverage as needed: Review and adjust coverage as needed. It's important to review your insurance policies regularly and to compare them with other options to ensure that you're getting the best coverage at the best price.
7. Keep in mind the government insurance options available: Keep in mind the government insurance options available such as Medicaid, Medicare and Obamacare.

In conclusion, choosing the right insurance plan can be overwhelming, but by assessing your needs, researching different options, comparing the benefits and costs, reading the fine print, consulting with a professional, reviewing and adjusting coverage as needed, and considering the government insurance options, individuals can make an informed decision about which plan is best for them. It's important to remember that insurance needs can change over time, so it's important to review and adjust coverage as needed. Additionally, it's important to make sure you have enough coverage to protect yourself and your assets and not to be swayed by low premium, as it could mean less coverage. By following these strategies, individuals can ensure that they have the right insurance coverage to protect themselves and their families in case of accidents, illness, or death.

CHAPTER SEVEN

The Financial Success Story: Conclusion

Long-term benefits of financial freedom

Financial freedom is the ability to live a life without worrying about money. It's the state of having enough wealth to meet one's needs and desires without having to work for a living. Achieving financial freedom can provide many long-term benefits, including:

1. Peace of mind: One of the most significant benefits of financial freedom is peace of mind. When individuals have enough money to meet their needs and desires, they don't have to worry about money and can focus on other things in life.
2. Time freedom: Financial freedom also provides time freedom. When individuals don't have to work for a living, they have the freedom to choose how they want to spend their time. This can include pursuing hobbies, traveling, or spending more time with family and friends.
3. Stress reduction: Financial stress can have a significant impact on an individual's overall well-being. Achieving financial freedom can reduce stress and improve overall health and happiness.
4. Ability to pursue passions: Financial freedom also allows individuals to pursue their passions. This can include starting a business, pursuing a career change or going back to school.
5. Ability to help others: Financial freedom also allows individuals to help others. They can give back to their community, support causes they care about, and help their loved ones.
6. Ability to plan for the future: Financial freedom also allows individuals to plan for the future. They can save for retirement, plan for their children's education, and make other long-term

financial plans.

7. Ability to build wealth: Achieving financial freedom also allows individuals to build wealth. This can include investing in real estate, stocks, or other assets that can grow in value over time.
8. Ability to enjoy life's pleasures: Financial freedom allows individuals to enjoy life's pleasures, such as traveling to different places, buying a house, buying a car, and more.
9. Ability to take risks: Financial freedom also allows individuals to take risks. They can start a business, invest in new ventures, and make other bold moves without worrying about the financial consequences.
10. Ability to leave a legacy: Financial freedom also allows individuals to leave a legacy. They can pass on their wealth to their children, create charitable foundations, and make other contributions that will outlast them.

In conclusion, Financial freedom is the ability to live a life without worrying about money. Achieving financial freedom can provide many long-term benefits such as peace of mind, time freedom, stress reduction, ability to pursue passions, help others, plan for the future, build wealth, enjoy life's pleasures, take risks, and leave a legacy. It's a lifelong process and requires discipline, planning, and persistence to achieve.

Taking action towards financial independence

Taking action towards financial independence is the first step towards achieving financial freedom. It requires discipline, planning, and persistence to make progress. Here are some strategies for taking action towards financial independence:

1. Set specific financial goals: Setting specific financial goals is the first step towards achieving financial independence. This includes setting short-term and long-term financial goals such as saving for a down payment on a house, paying off credit card debt, and saving for retirement.
2. Create a budget: A budget is a tool that helps individuals to track their income and expenses. It's important to create a budget and stick to it in order to achieve financial independence.
3. Save and invest: Saving and investing are essential for achieving financial independence. It's important to save a portion of each paycheck and invest the money in a diversified portfolio of assets.
4. Manage debt: Managing debt is an important part of achieving financial independence. It's important to pay off high-interest debt, such as credit card debt, as quickly as possible.
5. Build an emergency fund: An emergency fund is a savings account set aside for unexpected expenses. It's important to have an emergency fund in place to cover expenses in case of an unexpected event.
6. Increase income: Increasing income is an important part of achieving financial independence. This can be done through a variety of means such as taking on a side hustle, getting a raise,

or starting a business.

7. Track progress and stay motivated: Tracking progress and staying motivated is an important part of achieving financial independence. It's important to track progress towards financial goals, and to celebrate small wins along the way to stay motivated.
8. Get educated: Get educated about personal finance. Read books, attend seminars, and seek out other resources to learn more about personal finance and investing.
9. Be realistic and consistent: Be realistic about your financial goals and be consistent in working towards them. Recognize that achieving financial independence will take time and effort, but with persistence and discipline, it is possible to achieve.
10. Seek advice: Seek advice from financial professionals. Consult with a financial advisor, accountant or lawyer to help you make smart financial decisions.

In conclusion, taking action towards financial independence is the first step towards achieving financial freedom. It requires setting specific financial goals, creating a budget, saving and investing, managing debt, building an emergency fund, increasing income, tracking progress and staying motivated, getting educated, being realistic and consistent, and seeking advice from financial professionals. It's a lifelong process, it requires discipline, planning, and persistence to achieve, but with persistence and discipline, it is possible to achieve.

Recommended resources for further learning

Further learning is an important part of achieving financial independence. There are many resources available to help individuals learn more about personal finance and investing. Here are some recommended resources for further learning:

1. Books: There are many books available on personal finance and investing. Some popular books include "The Total Money Makeover" by Dave Ramsey, "Rich Dad, Poor Dad" by Robert Kiyosaki, "The Intelligent Investor" by Benjamin Graham and "The Credit Card Bible" by Anurag Yadav.
2. Online Resources: There are many online resources available on personal finance and investing, such as websites, blogs, and podcasts. Some popular websites include Dave Ramsey's website, Mr. Money Mustache, and The Simple Dollar.
3. Financial Advisors: A financial advisor can be a valuable resource for learning more about personal finance and investing. They can help individuals create a financial plan, invest their money, and answer any questions they may have.
4. Courses and Seminars: Courses and seminars can provide a comprehensive understanding of personal finance and investing. Some popular online learning platforms include Khan Academy, Coursera, and Udemy.
5. Financial Planning Organizations: Organizations such as the Financial Planning Association, the National Association of Personal Financial Advisors, and the Certified Financial Planner Board of Standards offer resources and educational opportunities to help individuals learn more about personal finance and investing.

6. Social Media: Social media platforms like Twitter, LinkedIn, and Facebook have many personal finance and investing experts that you can follow and learn from.
7. Retirement Planning calculators, Budgeting apps, and Investment tracking apps: These tools can help you to create a budget, track your expenses, and make investment decisions.
8. Networking: Networking with other individuals who have achieved financial independence can be a valuable resource for learning more about personal finance and investing.
9. Government websites: Government websites such as the Securities and Exchange Commission (SEC), the Financial Industry Regulatory Authority (FINRA), and the Consumer Financial Protection Bureau (CFPB) provide a wealth of information and educational resources to help individuals learn more about personal finance and investing.

In conclusion, there are many resources available to help individuals learn more about personal finance and investing. These include books, online resources, financial advisors, courses and seminars, financial planning organizations, social media, retirement planning calculators, budgeting apps, investment tracking apps, networking, and government websites. It's important to take advantage of these resources and continue to educate oneself about personal finance and investing in order to achieve financial independence. Additionally, it's important to keep in mind that personal finance is a lifelong process and it's important to continuously learn and adapt to changes in one's financial situation. By taking advantage of these resources and continuously learning, individuals can make informed decisions about their money and achieve financial independence.

Last Word

"Thank you for reading "Money Mastery: Achieving Financial Freedom at Any Age". We hope that this book has provided you with the information and strategies you need to make informed decisions about your money and achieve financial freedom in your 20s.

As a reminder, achieving financial freedom is a lifelong process and requires discipline, planning, and persistence. We encourage you to continue to educate yourself about personal finance and investing, and to adapt your strategies as your financial situation changes.

You can also connect with us on insta @real_anuragyadav

Once again, thank you for choosing this book. We wish you all the best in your journey towards financial freedom.

Best,

Anurag Yadav

P.S. If you have found this book helpful, please consider leaving a review on the platform from which the book has been purchased. Your feedback will help others find the book and benefit from the information it contains."

Your journey towards financial independence starts now,

thank you for joining us.

Printed by Libri Plureos GmbH in Hamburg,
Germany